Whales & Dolphins

Photo-Fact Collection

Scientific Consultant
Jennifer Gresham
Director of Education
Zoo New England

Copyright © 2013 Kidsbooks, LLC
3535 West Peterson Avenue
Chicago, IL 60659

Printed in China
101301001SZ

Visit us at **www.kidsbooks.com**

Humpback whale

CONTENTS

Living Large

It's amazing, but true. Some whales are even larger than the biggest dinosaurs were. Whales have lived on Earth for about 50 million years. As their food supply increased, whales ate more and became bigger over time. The blue whale is the largest animal that has ever lived. It can grow to 100 feet long and weigh about 300,000 pounds. That's as heavy as twenty-five elephants!

Humpback whale

Sounds Fishy

Although they live in water, whales and dolphins are not fish. They are cetaceans, a type of mammal. Like humans, they are warm-blooded. A thick layer of fat, called blubber, helps them keep warm and survive in the cold water. Also, cetaceans have lungs rather than gills. They breathe through blowholes at the top of their head. And, they don't hatch eggs; they give birth to their babies and then nurse them with milk.

Beluga whale

Humpback whales

What a Baby!

The baby humpback whale, swimming with its mother, might grow as long as 60 feet as an adult and weigh as much as 40 tons.

Gray whale

Tooth or Comb?

Cetaceans are grouped according to how they eat. Some have teeth that snag sea creatures. Others, like the big gray whale, have comblike structures called baleen. With baleen, whales can filter the seawater for food and eat thousands of pounds every day. No wonder they grow to such enormous sizes!

Totally Toothed

The majority of whales, including all dolphins and porpoises, have teeth. But they don't chew; they swallow their food whole. In fact, most toothed whales only use their teeth to catch and hold their prey. Orca teeth can be four inches long. They use them to grab seals right off the ice!

White Whale

Beluga whales favor shallow, coastal waters and use suction to capture prey. They suck in fish, squid, crabs, shrimp, clams, and worms.

Orca whale

Zap and Trap

Experts believe that the sperm whale produces sound waves from its large head, using echolocation to navigate the dark depths of the ocean to hunt. It may even use the sounds to stun its prey!

Sperm whale

Fast Feeders

Dolphins are very energetic swimmers, which helps them catch the 10 to 20 pounds of food they eat each day.

Common dolphin

Filter Feeders

It may seem odd, but there are 10 kinds of whales that don't have any teeth at all. Hanging from their upper jaws are rows of bristled strands called baleen. Made of a material similar to the human fingernail, the baleen acts as a food filter.

Humpback whale

baleen

Gulping Goodies

Fin whales, as well as blue, Bryde's, humpback, sei, and minke whales, are specially equipped to take huge gulps of krill and fish at one time. On their throats, there are grooves, or pleats, that stretch to allow the throat to expand.

Bryde's whale

Krill-a-Plenty

Many baleen whales feed on krill—orange sea creatures that look like shrimp and grow up to two inches long. Scientists estimate that there may be six and a half million tons in the Antarctic Ocean alone! A blue whale eats four tons of krill every day.

Humpback whale

Krill

Bubble Trouble

Because humpback whales prefer fish to krill, they sometimes eat in a special way, called bubble-net feeding. The humpback blows air from its blowhole as it swims in a spiral below a school of fish. The bubbles rise in a "net," surrounding the startled fish. The whale then swims inside the net of bubbles, catching the trapped fish.

11

It's a Fluke

One of the ways to tell whales apart is by their flukes. A sperm whale's huge, triangular flukes are 13 feet across.

A blue whale's 16-foot flukes are relatively small for such an enormous animal.

Humpbacks raise their flukes when diving. Humpback fluke patterns are like fingerprints. Scientists use them to tell individual whales apart.

Tales of Tails

Whales and dolphins propel themselves through the water with their tails, which have two strong wings, or flukes. Instead of wagging their flukes from side to side like fish, they move them up and down in powerful strokes.

umpback whale

Tall Tails

Dolphins have very strong tails that help them swim quickly, leap out of the water and tail-walk.

Bottlenose dolphin

Air Head

Looking at a whale, you wouldn't think it had a nose. But it does. Whales have nostrils, called blowholes. Over millions of years of evolution, whales' nostrils moved to the top of their head, allowing them to breathe by surfacing, rather than by sticking their whole head out of the water.

Air Holes

Baleen whales, like the gray whale, have two blowholes. The blowholes close up with muscular flaps when the whales dive, sealing out the water.

Gray whale

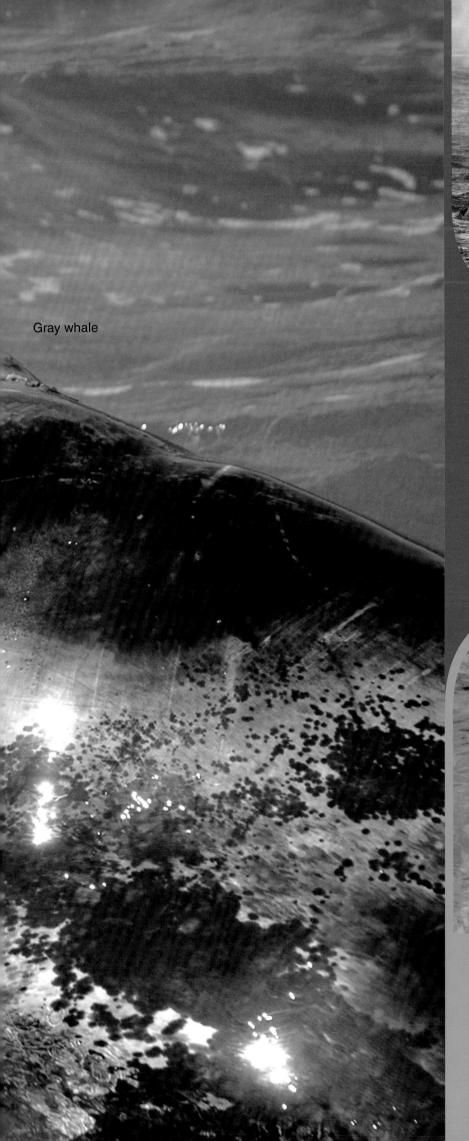

Gray whale

Gray whale

Spot the Spout

When a whale comes to the surface and exhales, water in the blowhole and moisture in the whale's breath burst into the air in a marvelous spout. Because whales have differently shaped blowholes, they have differently shaped spouts. The blow of a gray whale is shaped like a V.

Bottlenose dolphin

Smaller Spout

Toothed whales, like this dolphin, have only one blowhole. Because the dolphin is so small, it is very hard to see its spout. Large toothed whales, like a sperm whale, have a much larger blow.

Types of Whales & Dolphins

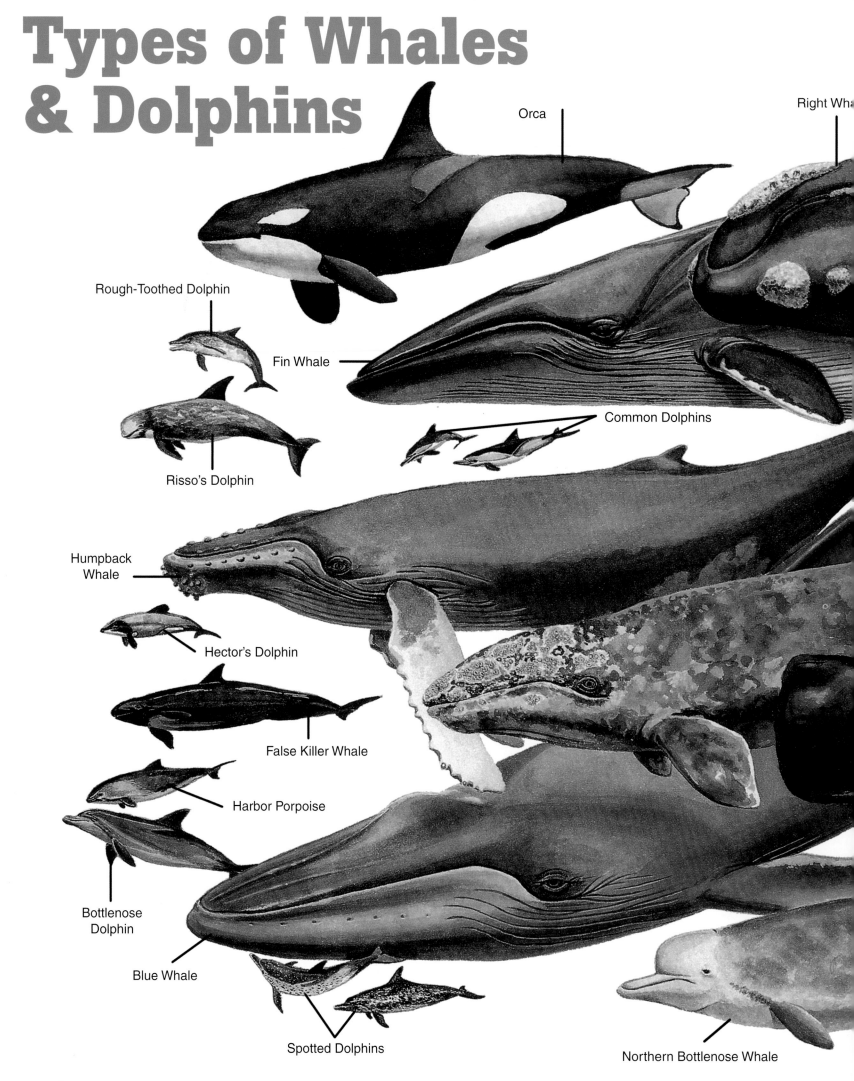

Orca

Right Wh

Rough-Toothed Dolphin

Fin Whale

Common Dolphins

Risso's Dolphin

Humpback Whale

Hector's Dolphin

False Killer Whale

Harbor Porpoise

Bottlenose Dolphin

Blue Whale

Spotted Dolphins

Northern Bottlenose Whale

Narwhal

Northern Right Whale Dolphin

Long-Finned Pilot Whale

Minke Whale

Gray
Whale

Amazon River Dolphin

Dall's
Porpoise

Beluga Whale

Dusky Dolphin

Sperm Whale

Striped Dolphin

Hourglass Dolphin

Pygmy Right Whale

Dynamic Dolphins

The dolphin family is made up of about 30 species of toothed whales, including the orca! They are fast swimmers, very intelligent, and are often found in groups, especially where there is a large concentration of food.

Bottlenose dolphins

Dolphins & People

People are drawn to dolphins, especially the way their snouts always make it look like they are smiling. We swim with them, put them in movies, and work with them on research about intelligence. These amazing animals are able to communicate with humans through squeaks, clicks, and body language.

Mother Love

Because they are mammals, a mother dolphin nurses her baby and takes care of it. A dolphin calf will often stay with its mother for three to six years.

Amazing Acrobats

Dolphins can jump over 10 feet out of the water in what is called a breach. They can also tail-walk and do other acrobatic movements.

Spyhopping

A spyhopping whale sticks its head straight out of the water like a giant periscope and holds it there for 30 seconds or more. It looks around, sometimes turning in a full circle, and then disappears. Then it sometimes comes back to do it all over again.

Humpback whale

Orca whale

Lobtailing

Without warning, a lobtailing whale suddenly points itself straight down into the water. It raises its huge flukes into the air, wags them playfully back and forth a few times, and then slaps them against the water with a sound as loud as a cannon shot.

Southern right whale

Water Sports

Whales, as big as they are, swim with unusual grace. But swimming is not all they can do. Whales perform aquabatics. They breach, lobtail, surf, and spyhop. Some scientists think that the noise made from lobtailing and breaching may be another way whales communicate. But maybe it's just whale's play.

Bottlenose dolphins

Racing and Chasing

Dolphins like to swim fast. When a speeding boat passes by, they'll race out in front and ride its bow waves. When racing each other, they'll first leap into the air and then take off after hitting the water. Dolphins also play tag and dance on their tails across the water's surface.

All in the Family

Most whales are fairly social and like to live in groups. These herds, or pods, vary in number and consist of family members and friends. Beluga whales usually live in Arctic waters in large groups that number up to 1,000. However, every few years one or two will follow cold currents as far south as New York City.

Beluga whale

Orca whales

Round-Trip Travelers

Many whales migrate constantly, traveling from one region to another to find food, breed, and have their young.

Calf

Home, Home on the Sea

Whales and dolphins live in all the world's oceans and some of its rivers, as well. Some live far out to sea while others hug the shore. Found in oceans from the tropics to the Arctic, orcas usually live in pods numbering three to thirty, but sometimes they travel in larger herds that number one hundred.

Common dolphins

HERD HUNGER

Group living is safer when enemies like sharks and killer whales are nearby. It also makes it easier for some whales to catch and find food. Species like the humpback whale sometimes gather in large groups and drive fish into a concentrated area. This is called cooperative feeding.

Humpback whales

Sea Sights & Sounds

Much of the sea is dark all of the time. To get around safely, find food, and to locate one another, whales and dolphins have developed keen senses. Many toothed whales, like the bottlenose dolphin, use echolocation to find their prey. Sound waves produced by the dolphin bounce off an object, like a school of fish. The waves bounce back, telling the animal where the fish are.

Bottlenose dolphin

A Real Water Melon

A whale's sounds probably originate in its nasal passages. The large forehead, or melon, found on some whales, like this bottlenose dolphin, is thought to focus the sounds. A beluga whale can change the shape of its melon when it produces sounds.

Beluga whale

Echo Vision

Like bats, toothed whales can make sounds to "see" what lies ahead. This sense is called echolocation. The dolphin's sound waves hit an object, such as a school of fish, and the echo bounces back. A bottlenose dolphin can make up to 1,000 clicking noises per second. Their large forehead, or melon, is thought to focus the sounds.

Bottlenose dolphin

Bottlenose dolphins

Underwater Ears

Although they have no ears on the outside of their heads, whales and dolphins have excellent hearing. Tiny pinholes, as narrow as a pencil, are located just behind their eyes. Through these holes, they can pick out sounds from many miles away.

Orca Antics

Like dolphins, orcas love to play. Although they can weigh as much as 18,000 pounds and grow to 32 feet, they are very athletic. Orcas can swim 30 miles per hour and can leap and turn quickly. These talents are what make them so dangerous. They fear nothing and can chase down almost any sea creature.

Fin Towers

How can you tell male and female orcas apart? Male orcas have really tall—up to six feet—dorsal fins. Females and young orcas have smaller, curved fins that resemble those of dolphins.

Male

Female

Lifetime Companions

Orca pods are very much like close families. An orca spends its whole life in the same group and continues to stay attached to its mother. Each pod may also have its own specific way of living, choosing to eat certain things and communicating in ways slightly different from other pods.

Life in Captivity

Orcas are very intelligent and can be trained for performances at marine parks. There is a lot of controversy about these shows and whether or not orcas should be in captivity.

Whales & People

Because of their size and speed, whales have few natural enemies besides humans. In the 19th century, people hunted whales to near extinction for oil, baleen, and meat. Baleen was used like plastic is today, in products like brushes and corsets. A few nations still practice whaling, but most have now stopped. Some whales are endangered, but most we just can't get enough information about to count their numbers.

Nylon Nick

Fishing lines and nets that float on the sea can severely injure dolphins and whales. The animal gets entangled, and the line cuts through its flesh. Rescue groups go out to cut the lines and save the whales.

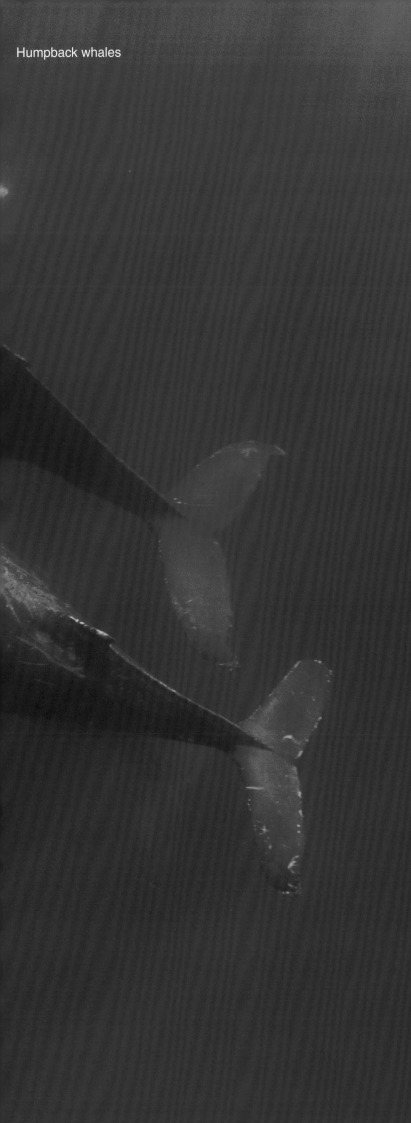

Humpback whales

Friendly Folks

Many scientists and other people and organizations are now working to secure a safer future for dolphins and whales. Stranding networks help beached animals get back into the water.

Pilot whale

Mammal Get-Together

Whale-watching groups go out to sea in hopes of seeing whales. These boats often work with scientists to help track whale movements.

GLOSSARY

Baleen: The rows of bristly bone in a baleen whale's jaw through which it filters food and water.

Baleen whale: A whale that has baleen rather than teeth in its mouth.

Blowhole: A nostril in the top of the head of a whale or other cetacean.

Blubber: Thick layer of fat that protects whales and other marine mammals from the cold.

Breach: To leap out of the water.

Bubble-net feeding: Style of feeding used by humpback whales in which the whale blows air from its blowhole to catch fish.

Calf: A baby or young whale.

Cetacea: Group of warm-blooded sea mammals that includes whales, dolphins, and porpoises.

Cooperative feeding: When whales or other animals gather in large groups and drive fish into a concentrated area to be eaten.

Dorsal fin: Large fin on the upper back of a fish that keeps the fish from rolling over.

Echolocation: A process of locating objects or food by making sound waves that bounce off the object and are reflected back to the animal making the sounds.

Fin: A stiff appendage on a whale or fish that helps it stay on course while swimming.

Fin whale: A type of whale—such as blue, Bryde's, humpback, and sei—that has a fin on its back and a specially pleated throat for feeding.

Flippers: The broad, flat limbs of whales used for steering, braking, and—sometimes—knocking away attackers.

Flukes: The two wings on the tails of whales and dolphins.

Krill: The tiny animals and plants living in the sea that are the basic food for larger sea animals; a type of plankton.

Lobtailing: When a whale points itself straight down into the water and raises its flukes into the air, then slaps them against the water.

Mammals: Animals that nourish their young with milk, such as whales and human beings.

Melon: The large forehead of some whales and dolphins.

Migration: An animal's move away from, or to, its breeding or feeding grounds at certain times of the year.

Navigate: To steer a course.

Pod: Herd of whales.

Sound waves: The pressure waves caused by audible or inaudible sounds.

Spout: A whale's exhalation ejected through its blowhole with force.

Spyhop: When a whale sticks its head out of the water and bobs on the surface.

Toothed whale: A whale that has teeth (rather than baleen).